The Autism Asperger Publishing Company is proud to be the sole U.S. publisher of this and a series of other carefully selected books on autism spectrum disorders originally published by the National Autistic Society (NAS) of Great Britain. To be faithful to the author, we have maintained the British spellings, punctuations, etc. However, to make for smoother reading and better understanding, in places we have deleted British terms and/or replaced them with their American equivalents.

Other NAS titles published by AAPC include:

- *Asperger Syndrome - Practical Strategies for the Classroom: A Teacher's Guide* by Leicester City Council and Leicestershire County Council
- *Challenging Behaviour in Autism: Making Sense - Making Progress: A Guide to Preventing and Managing Challenging Behaviour for Parents and Teachers* by Philip Whitaker
- *What is Asperger Syndrome and How Will it Affect Me? A Guide for Young People* by Martine Ives of the NAS Autism Helpline
- *Teaching Young Children with Autistic Spectrum Disorders to Learn: A Practical Guide for Parents and Staff in General Education Classrooms and Preschools* by Liz Hannah
- *The Other Half of Asperger Syndrome* by Maxine C. Aston
- *It Can Get Better* by Paul Dickinson and Liz Hannah

Fiona Bleach is an artist and illustrator. She works as an art therapist at The National Autistic Society's Sybil Elgar School in West London.

First published 2001 by The National Autistic Society, 393 City Road, London EC1V 1NG

ISBN 1-931282-06-4

Designed and typeset by Cottier & Sidaway

About this book

This book is aimed at young people who have
brothers or sisters with autism.

It is not about finding ways to make your brother or
sister change. Nor is it asking you to help in looking
after him or her. There are adults and professional
people specially trained to do that.

This book will help you understand autism and, in
doing so, you will be able to understand your brother
or sister better.

By understanding things, your life can become
easier. You will find it easier to manage the difficult
times, and time spent with your brother or sister will
be happier.

Introduction

If you are reading this book, it probably means that you know someone with autism.

It may be that you go to school with someone who has autism or, like many children around the world, you live with someone who has autism – your brother or sister, or brothers and sisters.

If this is you, then, whatever your age, you already have a greater understanding of autism than many adults.

Maybe you have felt confused and wonder why your brother or sister seems different and why he or she sometimes does strange things.

You are not alone!

Many adults find autism confusing and hard to understand, too, but we can learn from people with autism to help them live a life that is fun, full of love, satisfaction and happiness.

What is in this book?

Part 4
So how are you feeling?   49

Part 5
Special help – schools and therapies   63

Part 6
Glossary   73
(list of words to do with autism and what they mean)

Part 1
What is autism?

The word 'autism' comes from the Greek word 'autos', which means 'self'. This is because many people with autism often prefer to be by themselves.

If this is your brother or sister, he or she may seem to be in 'another world' and nothing else is important. Of course this is not true – you are important too!

Let us now take a look at autism and try to understand more before we talk about you.

General behaviour

The word 'autism' is used to describe the difficulties that your brother or sister may have, especially when he or she is with other people. Sometimes your brother or sister might have difficulties when he or she is alone, but it is usually when other people are around that problems arise.

People with autism sometimes have the same types of difficulties or the same ways of doing things. They may communicate differently, they may talk differently. They may talk 'at' you instead of "to" you. They may use sounds instead of words or not talk at all. They may have difficulties looking at you. They may need more time and help to learn things. They may dislike change.

Of course your brother or sister has his or her own personality and looks. He or she has certain likes and

dislikes as well as having autism. It is a bit like people being short-sighted – they need glasses to help them see better. Your brother or sister has autism, so he or she needs extra help to learn and understand better.

Why do some people have autism?

This is a question that is often asked, but nobody knows for sure.

There may be several different reasons or maybe just one. There are lots of different ideas about what causes autism.

Some people believe it is caused by damage to the brain before birth or that part of the brain has just developed differently. It may be that chemicals in the autistic person's brain are different to other people's brain chemicals.

Some people say that autism is 'genetic', it is in the 'genes'. This means that it is part of your brother or sister's characteristics, like having brown eyes or curly hair. Genetic means something that is decided in a person long before they are born and includes inherited characteristics from your parents. Autism is rarely

noticed in babies or very young children as it is hard to tell what small children have and have not learned. Usually, at about two or three years old, children with autism seem a bit different and learn at different speeds.

Again, it is a bit like needing glasses. Often, we cannot tell if babies or toddlers need glasses until they start reading or learning from books, usually after the age of two.

Whatever it is that causes autism, it is not anybody's fault. It is not your brother or sister's fault, not your parents' fault and not your fault.

Having autism does not mean that your brother or sister will have a shorter life than you. Autism is a 'developmental disability', not an illness. It relates to the physical workings inside the brain. This means it affects how someone 'develops' or learns.

Doctors, scientists and researchers are constantly looking for what might cause autism. Perhaps one day they will find an answer.

Epilepsy

Some people with autism also have a condition called 'epilepsy'.

Like autism, epilepsy can take many different forms. Epilepsy causes seizures. For some people, these seizures are brief and may cause them to black out. For other people, the seizures are more serious and may cause them to fall over, become unconscious and have spasms.

Anybody can have epilepsy – again, it is something to do with the brain and nothing to be worried about. There are books in your library that can give you more information on epilepsy.

Is there a cure for autism?

The answer to this question is no, not at the moment. Even though there is no cure, there are lots of ways in which you can help your brother or sister learn.

As a result of learning, he or she will be more able to enjoy life and get the most out of it. Schools, therapies and special ways of teaching all help (see Part 5). However, just being with you and your family will help your brother or sister learn to live with other people. This is real-life learning and it is often the most important.

It may be that your brother or sister will need lots of time and help to understand what is going on in the world. If he or she is feeling confused or frightened, your brother or sister might want to hide away or be alone. He or she might get frustrated because what is happening seems confusing and difficult to understand, even though it is all perfectly normal to you. Your brother or sister might get upset because he or she cannot explain to anyone that what is happening is frightening.

If all this seems confusing, do not worry! Autism is confusing for everybody – young people and adults alike.

Part 2
The three characteristics of autism

What are they?

There are three main areas that people with autism have difficulty with:

- the first is to do with **communicating**
- the second is to do with **making friends and being sociable**
- the third is to do with **imagination**.

Let's look at these areas one at a time.

Communicating

Perhaps your brother or sister does not speak or has difficulty in speaking.

He or she may take longer to understand the meanings of words or find too many words confusing. Things you find easy to understand may take longer for your brother or sister to learn.

Long sentences might be tricky for your brother or sister to understand or say. He or she may use one or two words instead of a sentence or else take your hand and show you instead of speaking because he or she is unable to say the right things.

Your brother or sister might have difficulty finding the right words or making the right sounds. Perhaps your brother or sister does not speak at all, pointing to what he or she wants or signing words with hands instead.

Communicating is also about facial expressions. This means we can understand how people are feeling by the looks on their faces.

You can tell if someone is cross or unhappy by the expression on his or her face, but your brother or sister may find it hard to understand these expressions. He or she may ignore them or copy them at the wrong time, perhaps pull strange faces for no reason or smile and laugh when you are unhappy. Your brother or sister is not being mean. It is just that they have not learned like you what to do with their faces, voices or words. He or she may get some bits right and some bits wrong. If your brother or sister does speak, it may sound a bit strange. People also use their bodies to 'talk' with. We use what are called 'gestures' – things like waving, winking, nodding,

pointing. These are all ways of talking without words. These movements may be clear to you, but are often confusing for your brother or sister. He or she may not understand the movements or miss them altogether.

Talking is full of hidden clues. The look on our faces might say what we are feeling, the sound of our voices change if we are joking or mad and we do lots of movements with our hands and bodies without realizing it.

All of these things can be overwhelming for someone with autism. They can also be frustrating and upsetting.

Your brother or sister may feel frustrated because he or she cannot understand what people are saying or what they want and may feel alone because he or she cannot join in. This may be why your brother or sister prefers not to be involved with talking at all!

Making friends and being sociable

This is about taking an interest in other people, sharing, playing, helping. Your brother or sister may have difficulties with 'social' things and making friends.

Because your brother or sister may not understand conversation or games, he or she may find it is easier to be alone in his or her own 'safe' world. This world is safe because he or she is in charge of what happens and it is familiar.

This familiar world may not always include you or your family or friends.

Why not? Because you all keep moving about and doing different things!

Your brother or sister does not know what you are going to do or say next, and this can be worrying! He or she may be startled if someone suddenly coughs or sneezes or by the sound of sudden laughter from someone while quietly watching television. Even the sound of someone turning the pages of a newspaper might be upsetting. These normal, everyday things might be so distressing for your brother or sister that he or she feels the need to hide his or her head or run off.

Imagine what it would feel like to be in a silent room with sudden, strange noises coming from nowhere. Loud noises, quiet noises, laughter, movement and people suddenly standing up and sitting down for no reason that you can understand. You might be worried too!

Maybe this is how 'ordinary life' sometimes feels for your brother or sister.

Your brother or sister may not understand about manners or being polite. He or she may not understand sharing or taking turns.

When we are young, most of us learn how to behave 'nicely' with friends and other people. We cannot do or have everything we want and we should not take things that do not belong to us. If we do, we risk people not liking us. We also know that we would not like things taken from us – we can understand how it feels.

Your brother or sister finds it hard to understand other people's feelings and he or she may not realize that taking something that belongs to someone else can be very annoying and upsetting for others. Your brother or sister may not mind people not wanting to be friends. He or she may prefer to be by him or herself anyway and not understand what friends are for.

Your brother or sister is probably totally unaware that he or she has done anything wrong or caused any upset.

It may be hard for your brother or sister to understand turn-taking or to play games by the rules. He or she may not understand what rules are for or have any interest in winning. Even throwing and catching a ball

might seem pointless to your brother or sister. It may
not be his or her idea of fun.

Your brother or sister might need lots of time and help
to be able to play with you or other children.

Sharing toys, candy and drinks is something that your
brother or sister might find extra hard! We all have
difficulties with sharing sometimes, even as adults!
Your brother or sister might become so attached to
something that giving it up may seem like a life or
death situation. Also, your brother or sister might think
that when he or she gives something away, it is gone
forever. He or she might not realize that a ball will be
thrown back or that there will be chocolate cookies
again tomorrow.

It may be that your brother or sister can only think of
the very moment he or she is in, not of the future and
not of the past.

Being 'sociable' is hard work!

Imagination

Your brother or sister may find it hard to imagine what it is like to be you.
It may be difficult for him or her to see the world from your point of view, so perhaps he or she ignores anything you do or say or seems to think it is unimportant. Your brother or sister may appear to find your hobbies boring. He or she may not understand you or your interests because he or she has difficulty understanding the world he or she lives in, let alone the world you live in!

Sometimes it might seem that your brother or sister is being rude or selfish. He or she might turn off the television while you are watching or walk off halfway through a conversation. Your brother or sister does not realize that this seems rude or selfish because he or she does not understand that it upsets you. It is hard for your brother or sister to understand his or her own feelings, so you can imagine how hard it must be to understand your feelings. He or she may not even realize that you have feelings!

It may also be difficult for some people with autism to imagine that other people have their own families, homes and lives to live. They may think that other people just disappear when they are out of sight. They may not even question where they go.

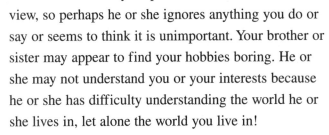

Sometimes people with autism only speak to their family, friends and teachers when they are in their 'proper' places – to their families at home, friends and teachers at school, doctors in hospital and so on. It does not make sense to them to see these people in different places – that is, not where they 'belong'.

Sometimes that feeling can happen to us. You may see the postman every day for years and know his face well, then one day you swim past him in the swimming pool and think 'Who's that waving to me?!'

So, the three areas that we have talked about are:
- communicating
- making friends
- imagining

and they are often the most difficult things for people with autism to do. You may recognize some of these things as being difficult for your brother or sister.

Remember:
- help and support can be given to *all* people with autism so that they are able to learn in their own way and in their own time. No one is beyond being able to learn.

Part 3
Odd behaviour

What's going on?

This chapter will try to help you understand why your brother or sister sometimes does strange things.

People with autism often do things very suddenly and it can seem that there is no reason for what they are doing, which can be very alarming. There either is no reason or it is hard to find out what it is – like trying to understand why some people actually like bungee jumping!

If you know the person very well, then it becomes easier to understand what he or she does.

There is always a reason behind behaviour, even though we cannot always see it! Maybe you have tried to work out some answers for yourself.

By living with your brother or sister you already know a lot about autism without realizing it.

Let us take a look at some of the types of behaviour people with autism might have. Then we will try to work out why some of these things are happening.

Why does my brother or sister not speak?

Some people with autism never speak at all. Others perhaps started talking when they were young, then stopped suddenly. Why this is so, nobody knows for sure. Researchers are constantly trying to discover the causes.

Maybe the part of the brain where speech is controlled changes at a certain age and so develops differently, affecting speech.

Perhaps these people with autism 'choose' not to speak. They may find speech meaningless. If they have difficulties learning what words mean, they cannot understand what other people are saying. They may therefore feel that there is no reason to use words to talk back. Language becomes unnecessary and pointless to them.

Often other methods of communication are taught when people with autism do not speak at all. They might use their hands to sign words or point to special pictures known as 'symbols'. Most young people can learn these signs and symbols, and most schools use them for special needs learning.

Everyone is unique and we all have individual ways of communicating. Some people use their hands a lot, some people talk very quietly, others use their faces (with expression) to show what they mean.

If your brother or sister does not speak, or speaks very little, the school may work out an individual 'communicating programme'. Maybe he or she will have signs and symbols on a key ring, so your brother or sister can point to what he or she needs. Perhaps he or she will have a little book of photographs of people and places.

There are endless ways of helping people communicate. Different things suit different people. Computers and changing technology are helping all the time.

Why does my brother or sister make strange noises?

Your brother or sister may make strange noises because he or she has difficulty making word sounds. When your brother or sister hears other people speaking, it may sound jumbled and confusing, so he or she talks back in strange jumbled sounds or noises.

Imagine being in a foreign country where everyone speaks a language you do not know. You might try to copy what you think are the right sounds and words without knowing the meaning of them just to join in! If you found it too hard you might not talk at all.

The noises could be your brother or sister's own invented way of talking. The sounds may mean 'I need help', 'I don't want to do it', 'I'm hungry' and so on. It may be hard to work out what your brother or sister is trying to say, unless you know the sounds well.

Perhaps your brother or sister finds his or her own sounds interesting. He or she may enjoy experimenting with different noises, a bit like an opera singer practising!

Why does my brother or sister repeat things I say?

Repeating words or sentences is called 'echolalia', which comes from the word 'echo'. This word is used because your brother or sister is actually echoing what he or she hears.

This may be his or her way of communicating because it is easier than finding the right words to say. Your brother or sister may feel as though he or she is having a normal conversation as he or she is using words that you understand. So, you may hear your brother or sister say, 'He wants a sandwich', meaning, 'I want a sandwich' or, 'She doesn't want to go', meaning, 'I don't want to go.'

Everyone is different, so the better you know your brother or sister, the easier it will be to understand his or her way of communicating.

Why does my brother or sister ask the same question over and over again?

Asking the same question or saying the same sentence again and again can be very exhausting to listen to! Try to stay calm – eventually the conversation will move on.

Your brother or sister may need to keep asking the same thing as he or she wants to hear the same answer each time. Maybe when your brother or sister is anxious or upset he or she asks the same question more often. Your brother or sister may have to keep asking because his or her anxiety gets in the way of being able to 'hear' the answer. In other words, the answer is not sinking in.

The same question is usually followed by the same answer, which makes your brother or sister feel safe. It is something that he or she can rely on in an unpredictable world. Because of this, he or she will not want to hear a different answer. Your brother or sister may enjoy the rhythm of repeating words. This repetition may be comforting, like a favourite song or chant.

Why does my brother or sister talk to him or herself?

This is quite common for people with autism – and sometimes for other people too! You may find it more noticeable when your brother or sister is enjoying being alone. Really, it is just thinking aloud.

We all talk to ourselves from time to time, even if it is just shouting out loud when we drop something. We tend to do it more as we get older or maybe when we are trying to remember lists or numbers. Singing to ourselves is more common and, for some reason, more acceptable.

The difference is, we usually try not to do it if other people are around so if someone talks to themselves at other times it seems odd. Your brother or sister may simply not be aware of other people or not be concerned about what other people think. Perhaps it is actually a strength, to be this unconcerned.

Why does my brother or sister like to be alone?

Perhaps your brother or sister likes to spend time alone. This does not mean that he or she does not like you or other people. It may simply be that your brother or sister needs lots of time to think quietly by him or herself.

Perhaps your brother or sister sometimes finds other people too noisy, too quiet, too confusing. Perhaps lots of movement and sound is overwhelming for him or her. Remember, lots of people with autism like to know what is coming next. Even ordinary conversations and games can sometimes feel frightening because they do not know what they or others are going to do or say next.

Imagine for a moment that we are all in a play. We would all know our lines and what everyone else was going to say or do next. People with autism might find this an easier situation to be in, because it is planned and predictable.

Of course, life is not like that – we make things up as we go along, and this is part of the fun of life, meeting new people, doing new things. For your brother or sister, these things could be worrying. Maybe it is like sitting in a dentist's waiting room – something is going to happen but you don't know what!

Because your brother or sister does not know what people are going to do next, he or she may prefer to be alone. Perhaps your brother or sister likes to be alone because he or she does not share the same interests as you. He or she may have particular, unusual interests and need lots of time to do them.

Sometimes people with autism like lining things up or arranging objects in certain ways. They may like drawing the same thing over and over again or tapping things together. Although this might not be your idea of fun, it is a comforting and safe thing for your brother or sister because he or she is in control of it. Being alone to do these things means there is no fear of interruption. Being interrupted halfway through something can be very frustrating for anyone!

Why does my brother or sister like doing the same things over and over again?

Perhaps your brother or sister likes lining up objects in the same order or switching lights on and off before he or she goes into a room. Maybe he or she has to take the same route whenever going out or put his or her clothes on in exactly the same order.

All of these things are common in people with autism and this pattern is called 'ritualistic behaviour'. A 'ritual' is a ceremony or action that is done exactly the same each time, like a wedding service or even a particular way and time of brushing your teeth.

Your brother or sister may need to do things exactly the same each time because he or she feels 'safe' and 'in control' by doing this.

He or she may feel that if he or she does these things, the rest of the day will go all right. It is a bit like crossing your fingers for good luck or taking a 'lucky charm' to an exam with you. Though it probably will not change what happens, it makes you feel better and safer. Some people always wear a special item of jewelery, maybe a gift given to them by a loved one. Wedding rings can make people feel safe and loved. These things all make us feel better for whatever reason.

In the same way, your brother or sister could feel better when he or she does certain things in certain ways – ways that have gone well before. Any interference or change can be difficult for him or her because it is new and risky and could be full of nasty surprises!

Again, this may be hard to understand, but, in fact, we all have little rituals that we like to do. It could be kissing all the family goodbye in the same order, sitting on the same seat to watch television or the same place on a bus or eating certain meals on certain days of the week.

We like to stick to these things because they are familiar – that is, we know them well and feel good about them. It is the same for your brother or sister. It makes him or her feel better, it creates a nice safe feeling.

Of course, these odd routines might seem annoying or pointless to other people, but, remember, your brother or sister is not trying to be awkward. He or she does not realize that it might be annoying for others or why you do the things you do!

Why does my brother or sister jump, rock, tap, flap or spin?

Children and adults with autism sometimes spend time spinning, rocking or repeating movements with their bodies. Some like to twist, turn or tap objects, or flick things in front of their eyes. Others might rock back and forth from foot to foot.

All of these things usually happen when your brother or sister has free time and is not busy with other activities.

These things might feel relaxing and comforting to your brother or sister. It is a chance to just be him or herself and enjoy the repeated movements or sounds. Your brother or sister might find it enjoyable because he or she is in control of what is happening and knows what is coming next – the same thing.

Perhaps your brother or sister does these things more when happy and excited. It could be his or her way of showing delight. Think of soccer players when they score goals – we see all sorts of ways to express delight then! Some punch the air, others do little dances, some skid along on their knees – these are all ways of saying 'Great!' without using words.

We think this is 'normal' behaviour on the football pitch because it is part of the game and having fun. However, we do not expect our doctors to jump up and down if they cure us!

Your brother or sister might not realize that people behave differently in different situations. He or she has not learned the rules for how to behave in order to fit in. Perhaps he or she does not care about fitting in and does not worry about what other people think. Perhaps we worry too much.

Spinning, rocking and flapping hands might feel good to your brother or sister. Carnival rides create this feeling, so does jumping on a trampoline and going up and down in elavators. It could be that your brother or sister is finding his or her own ways of feeling these sensations.

Sometimes these movements are comforting and calming, like rocking a baby to sleep or bouncing toddlers on your knee. Think how relaxing and peaceful being on a swing on a warm summer's day can feel. Swinging creates a feeling that people with autism recreate by rocking and so on.

Why will my brother or sister not look at me?

As mentioned before, when we talk to people we use much more than just our voices. Our hands, bodies and the expressions on our faces are communicating all the time. We could even answer a simple question by not speaking, just using our eyebrows!

There is something else, though, something we constantly use without even thinking about it. It is a part or our body that reveals the most about how we feel – our eyes.

When we talk or listen to people, we make contact with our eyes. We can see if the other person is interested in us, we can work out how they are feeling, we can predict what they have in mind. Our eyes give clues as to whether we are joking, serious, angry or sad.

Looking directly at people, looking into their eyes, is called making 'eye contact'. Because some people with autism do not make much eye contact, they may miss all these little signs.

Not all people with autism find eye contact difficult, but lots do.

Sometimes, shy people hold their heads down to avoid making eye contact. By doing this, they do not give too much of themselves away. Other people cannot work out how they are feeling or what they are thinking. It also means that conversations tend to be short.

Perhaps your brother or sister is a bit like this. He or she does not want other people to know too much about him or her in case this will create the expectation of having a conversation. Making eye contact is something we usually do when we are introduced to other people, then conversations can take place.

For some people eye contact is uncomfortable and awkward. By looking directly at people, it means we have to accept them into our world and accept that they, too, exist.

Perhaps this part is difficult for your brother or sister. By making eye contact with you, he or she might have to start thinking about your feelings. As mentioned before, people with autism have difficulty in doing this as their own feelings are often overwhelming and confusing, let alone working out anyone else's. So, thinking about you may just add to their problems.

Why does my brother or sister cover his or her ears, eyes or head?

Some people with autism like to spend time alone. If your brother or sister wants to be alone, but cannot be because he or she is in a car, shopping centre or a playground, for example, he or she may wish or want to block out the world and pretend that no one else is there.

A way to block the world out could be to pull his or her coat up over his or her head, another could be to cover the ears with his or her hands.

People with autism are very smart in thinking up ways to help themselves cope in a world that is constantly changing. So, by covering themselves, they may be telling you that they do not want to join in at that moment.

Some people with autism have very good hearing and so may be sensitive to noises. This means that some sounds, even quiet ones, or sounds that are far away, might be upsetting or painful for your brother or sister to hear. He or she may therefore, quite naturally, want to protect him or herself by covering the ears.

We often hear of people who hate the sound of fingernails being scratched down a board. Well, maybe some sounds that seem ordinary to us feel just as horrible to your brother or sister!

Why does my brother or sister not like change?

Lots of people are not keen on change, not just those with autism. Change means that something is ending. We sometimes forget that this means something new is beginning – it is not just about losing what we know.

New things may be frightening at first. Have you ever felt this? Think about moving up a class at school. You might worry about:

- your new teacher – will he or she be nice?
- new work – will I be able to do it?
- new classroom – where is it?

We might find ourselves longing for the old things we know – we know how to deal with them, what to expect.

People with autism might feel like this about all change. Little changes for us might be huge for your brother or sister. He or she will want things to stay the same, not wanting to go to a new restaurant, for example, but to the one you always have been to in the past. Why is this?

Because we understand some of the world we live in, we know that change has to happen all the time and we get used to it. We know that some changes are fine and will not harm us – they can actually make things better. We know, too, that if we do not understand what is happening we can ask other people to explain.

Because people with autism have difficulty in learning and understanding, they may not be able to ask, they may think that any change means everything is going to change.

Imagine how it might feel if, when you are given a different-coloured cup, you think, 'Does this mean I will have a different Mom and Dad, a different home?'

To you, a blue cup is followed by dinner, play, television, wash and bed. Fine. What, though, panic, panic, does a red cup mean?!!

Your brother or sister may not be able to ask about change or even understand that change is going to happen until it is actually starting. So, going to a new café for your brother or sister could be like waking up in a completely different bedroom would be for you. It could be that confusing and upsetting.

You would probably panic and search for the what you know – the wallpaper you chose and toys you know, and the bed by the window. In the same way, your brother or sister might want the old café with the curtains he or she likes or the toilets with blue doors!

Imagine you are suddenly in this new bedroom and not able to ask any questions about it or why you are there. Imagine not understanding anything anyone is saying. Understandably, real panic might set in, followed by despair, crying and utter confusion.

This is how change might always feel to your brother or sister. He or she is confused in a very confusing world. For this reason, anything recognizable or familiar might be a great comfort.

Why does my brother or sister throw or break things?

People with autism sometimes throw objects. It may seem strange that your brother or sister could even throw or break the things that are very special to him or her. It could be a favourite toy or book, it could be something that cannot be mended, like a camera or calculator, or it could simply be something that is close by.

Why does this happen?

Well, we have to think about when it happens. Perhaps your brother or sister has been asked to do something that he or she does not understand or something that is too hard. It might be that, by getting rid of the object, he or she does not have to do it. Perhaps it is simply his or her way of saying, 'No, I don't like it, I don't want it!'

If your brother or sister sometimes throws things at you, try not to be upset. This may be his or her only way of letting you know how he or she feels. It might be a 'leave me alone' or 'go away' throw or a way of getting attention – your attention or that of the family or a friend. Your brother or sister might know that if he or she throws or smashes

something, everyone will suddenly stop what they are doing and go to him or her. This is called 'negative attention'. Although he or she knows people will be mad, it is better than not getting any attention at all!

Sometimes it is the result of just plain frustration and anger! If your brother or sister wants to tell you something but does not know how to, it could be very upsetting, especially if it is something that is important to him or her.

Imagine being in a foreign country where you do not speak the language and you have a wasp stuck in your ear. How would you let people know what was wrong? How could you get help? How upset and angry would you feel towards the people around

you? You might lose your temper, scream, shout and throw things in despair! Maybe this is how it feels for someone with autism who is trying to tell us something.

Do not forget that people with autism might not be able to think about what happens after they have thrown something, that a toy or calculator is smashed forever.

There is always a reason for your brother or sister throwing things, even if we cannot see what that reason is. It is often hard to recognize why it happens, but, remember, it is not your fault, nor is it your brother or sister's fault. Perhaps he or she is just trying to let you know something.

Why does my brother or sister hurt other people?

There may be times when your brother or sister feels so angry and upset that the only thing he or she can do is take it out on someone else.

Your brother or sister may hurt the person standing nearest – you, if you are unlucky enough, or maybe a certain person he or she has hit before.

Searching for the same person – be it a friend, teacher or member of the family – is often called 'targeting'.

Your brother or sister may target the same person whenever he or she is upset. This can seem really unfair, especially when that person is not involved in the situation and may even be in another room.

This does not mean that your brother or sister really dislikes the unfortunate person – it is usually because he or she has done it before and it has become a habit. Remember, people

with autism like things to be the same. This may even mean hurting the same person every time.

Often, for people with autism, hitting or hurting others may be the only way they have to express their unhappiness. It is their way of saying, 'Go away!' 'I don't want it!' or 'Let me have it!'

If we want to change a situation, we can think up lots of reasons for us being given our own way. We may even lie to get things we want. Your brother or sister might not be able to do this, so force may be the only way he or she knows to achieve this.

Sometimes we can clearly see what causes an upset, such as being told it is time to go to bed. Other times, there may seem to be no reason at all. It could be that your brother or sister is remembering something upsetting or perhaps is reminded of something he or she does not like, maybe a certain piece of music or a cough.

Try not to be too upset if you get hurt – your brother or sister is not really angry with you. He or she just has not learned other ways to express feelings. Ask your parents or teachers to help you look for ways to change this hurtful behaviour.

Why does my brother or sister hurt him or herself?

Sometimes children and adults with autism hurt themselves deliberately. This is known as 'self-harming' or 'self-injurious' behaviour.

Seeing your brother or sister doing this might be very upsetting and confusing for you. You might feel scared and worried. Remember, there are adults, teachers, carers, parents and doctors who are there to help your brother or sister.

It is not up to you to try to stop your brother or sister hurting him or herself. It is not your fault if it happens. Your brother or sister has a special difficulty and he or she is dealing with it in a special way.

Of course, your brother or sister might never do this, but it is worth knowing about as it does happen. You may also meet other children with autism who do this.

So, what are common ways of self-harming?

- Some people with autism bite the backs of their hands or other parts of their body.
- Some bang their heads against a wall or other hard surface.
- Some people with autism hit themselves.
- Some people scratch themselves.
- Some people with autism pull their hair.

These things usually happen when people with autism are very unhappy. They could be feeling very confused, frightened, tense and frustrated. They could be in physical pain, but are unable to communicate this. Perhaps they have spent ages trying to 'say' something without using words and nobody understands. Maybe they feel alone, frightened and helpless, but cannot explain this to anyone. They may simply have been asked to do something that is just too much for them. Remember, it might be small to us, but huge for them.

Perhaps by hurting him or herself, your brother or sister is able to block out unhappy thoughts. It may take his or her mind off something too upsetting to think about. Perhaps your brother or sister feels so tense and worried that the only way of releasing this tension is to hurt him or herself physically. This might be the only way he or she knows to express distress.

Similar behaviour (but far less damaging) can sometimes be seen in nervous people. You may know someone who nibbles their nails, twists and pulls their hair or bites their lip to stop themselves crying.

We all get upset and angry from time to time. We all do things to help us cope with our feelings.

Some people stamp their feet, bang their fists, jump up and down and shout. Others get red in the face, point their fingers and hit things. These are all ways of coping with a difficult situation. What do you do?

Some scientists believe that when we hurt ourselves, chemicals in the brain change to help us recover. Maybe people with autism can feel this chemical change and it makes them feel better.

Why is my brother or sister very good at some things and finds easy things so hard?

Sometimes people with autism have special talents. It could be solving electrical problems, putting together difficult jigsaws or singing in perfect pitch. It might be drawing extremely well, playing a musical instrument or remembering lots of numbers and dates. They may be able to do these things even when they are very young.

Your brother or sister might not realize that he or she is smart or has great skills. People with autism sometimes have these skills without having to learn or work hard to get them. They may find having a conversation or buying something from a shop much harder than playing a violin like a professional soloist!

Why is this? Well, nobody knows for sure, but perhaps it is to do with the ways different parts of the brain work.

As mentioned earlier, things that you find easy – like talking to friends, going shopping – might take a long time for your brother or sister to learn. Yet, for a few people with autism, things that we find hard – like remembering dates, calculating numbers and playing musical instruments – are very natural and do not need years of learning in the usual way to make them possible.

Not all people with autism have these special skills – in fact, only a very small number do.

We are all different – we are all important.

Why does my brother or sister always get his or her own way?!!

This does not really happen every time, it is just that people with autism need different rules to help them overcome their difficulties. You may understand more and may be more responsible than your brother or sister, so it is important that you live within the ordinary rules in society.

Part 4
So how are you feeling?

We know that if you live with or share part of your life with someone with autism there are times when things get difficult. Because of the autism, your Mom, Dad, relatives, adult friends or whoever looks after you probably have to give more time to your brother or sister. Because autism is such a complicated disability, they may be left feeling exhausted!

What you might be experiencing

Maybe you sometimes feel left out, ignored, lonely, angry, frustrated or upset. There may be times when you feel so angry towards your brother or sister, you wish he or she did not exist.

Do not worry – these feelings are normal. We all lose our temper, we all get angry and we all think rotten things about other people from time to time. This is all part of normal family life.

Normal family life can be tricky for anyone in any family. If someone in your family has autism, it can be extra complicated.

Why, you may ask? Because you may be expected to do things by yourself, to organize what you need, get yourself ready.

Your Mom, Dad or whoever looks after you might expect you to sometimes act older than you actually are. Maybe to even act older and more responsible than an older brother or sister with autism! This may seem unfair, but, remember, your brother or sister may think it unfair that everything comes so easily to you and that you are more independent than he or she is able to be.

As was said earlier, people with autism need lots of time and help from everyone so that they can understand the world they are in.

Your Mom, Dad, teachers and others are constantly thinking up new ways to help your brother or sister learn. What works today may not work tomorrow. This can be very tiring for everyone.

It is very important that you know that you are not less important than your brother or sister or less loved, it is just that people rely on you and trust you to do things by yourself because your brother or sister needs more time to do even the simple, everyday things. So, you may be expected to look after yourself more, be more independent, more responsible, more sensible than you want to be.

You may be asked to help your brother or sister when all you want to do is have fun. It is hard for anyone, at any age, to always be sensible and responsible. In a way, people expect more of you

just because you have a brother or sister with autism. It is perfectly understandable that you could well find this infuriating!

What you can do

Start by thinking about what you want. Then, talk about it!

It is important to let other people know how you are feeling. If your feelings are bottled up inside you, nothing can change – people will think you are fine with the situation.

Write down what you would like to see change. Keep a list of things that work well and things that irritate you. Do not try to write it all at once as it will be hard to remember everything. Rather, add to the list when situations arise. Do not try to think of solutions either – there will be time to do that later with your family. Write down everything that occurs during a day that you feel is unfair, too demanding, out of your control or upsetting for you.

Try to use the list in a positive way, too – point out things that work well, then look at the things that need changing. Think about what could be altered to help you.

In helping you, the whole family will benefit as a more positive environment will be created.

If you want time with your parents, talk to them about it. They are not mind-readers and may simply not have noticed that you are feeling frustrated!

Discuss your needs and try to agree on a certain time every week that is 'your time'.

This should be uninterrupted and regular. This is 'your time' with your Mom, Dad or whoever looks after you. Try not to cancel or miss this time – it needs to become part of the normal week.

If 'your time' does become a regular thing, your brother or sister will recognize the routine and, after a while, be able to accept it.

If your brother or sister is not too demanding of attention or support, he or she will take to this routine well. If you have difficulties finding a place to talk or if your brother or sister is very demanding and keeps interrupting, think of other places where you can have 'your time'.

Could you go for a walk or to a coffee shop with your Mom, Dad or other member of your family one afternoon or evening every week? If you are out of the house altogether, it may make it easier for your brother or sister as well as yourself.

At first, your brother or sister might have difficulties in accepting this new routine and feel upset and rejected. Keep 'your time' short to start with, so he or she realizes that you have not gone forever – you will be back!

On your return, give praise and make a fuss of your brother or sister, so he or she knows that everything is fine and you still want to be with him or her.

Do not give up, even if it means setting the pattern very gradually.

The first week, 'your time' might have to be as short as five minutes. The second week it could be 15 minutes, then half an hour and so on, until you are able to spend long stretches of time with one of your parents or caregivers.

Eventually, your brother or sister will learn that this is 'your time' and that you are important, too! If they do have difficulties with it, be patient – change can be upsetting.

No time to yourself?

We all need time alone. It is an important part of our lives. We need time to gather our thoughts together, make decisions or think about our feelings. Some people enjoy spending a lot of time alone, whether in work, play or just thinking.

If this is you, do not feel guilty about it. Most inventions, scientific discoveries, books, music, art and a whole lot of other things have been created by people working and thinking alone.

It is not unreasonable to want time to yourself. You are not being selfish and you are not being mean to your brother or sister if you sometimes need to get away.

Try to achieve a balance between time spent with your family and time spent alone. This could become a daily routine. Remember, setting a routine or a schedule for your day will make it easier for your brother or sister to respect your wishes. This is because then he or she will be able to predict when you will not be around. For example, you could announce to the family or stick a note on the fridge saying, 'From 5 o'clock to 6 o'clock

every day, I want to spend time alone.' By explaining this clearly, especially to your brother or sister, it is more likely to happen.

If he or she has difficulty in understanding, be inventive! Draw a clock face with moving hands or use an alarm clock to show when the hour is up. Set the clock so that when the beep goes off, your time alone is finished. Another way is to explain that the music of a certain TV show, at a certain time, is a signal that your time alone has finished. Your brother, sister, Mom, Dad or other members of your family can then join you.

Your parents need to respect the time you spend alone as well. Discuss your need for regular time alone and agree on times when this will be possible.

Do not forget, if it is impossible to spend time alone at home, use your imagination. Find your own way of getting away from it all! What about libraries, coffee shops, neighbours or maybe supervised times after school?

Be patient. Start slowly so routines can be set. Routines then become recognized, and recognition means respect!

No privacy?

Privacy is important for everyone, of any age. We need to respect other people's privacy and have ours respected, too.

From an early age, even young children seem to have an idea about what is private. We are taught by our elders, our teachers and our friends that some things are private, even though we all do them. Perhaps if we were not taught this, there would be no concern for privacy.

Other countries and cultures have different ideas about what is and is not private. In some countries, burping after a meal expresses thanks and approval. In others, sneezing in public is considered revolting!

To some extent, we all want to be part of the society we grow up in. Most of us have a natural need to fit in and follow the basic rules, manners and behaviour of our country. If we do not, we risk being disliked and avoided.

Respecting your privacy and respecting his or her own privacy are things your brother or sister might have difficulty with. He or she might not have learned or understood that some behaviour is inappropriate in public. Your brother or sister might barge in while you are washing or dressing, not realizing that this is a problem for you. He or she might use the toilet without closing the door and expect you to do the same. Your brother or sister might need to be taught again and again about privacy and always need reminding.

Try not to get angry or upset if you are disturbed during private activities. Your brother or sister is not prying or being disrespectful – he or she is probably unaware of any embarrassment. Try to keep it light-hearted as you redirect him or her.

Try using the same expression whenever you are interrupted, such as 'No thank you, close the door please, this is private.'

If your brother or sister is unable to respect your private or personal possessions, get a box with a padlock or combination lock. This way you can keep your letters, school work, special toiletries, books and games safe.

Try to avoid having a lock on your bedroom door – this could be a risk to your safety in emergencies. It is better to keep reminding your brother or sister about privacy than having to lock yourself away.

It may take time for your brother or sister to understand and accept, so use your imaginative skills to help this along. Stick photographs of yourself on your boxes, your cupboards, your toothbrush, your bed and so on, and do the same for his or her things. Show your brother or sister what is his or hers and what is yours. This will help your brother or sister understand and feel important.

Be patient. Be inventive. Be clever!

While helping yourself, make it fun for your brother or sister – you are more likely to get positive results that way.

Does your brother or sister embarrass you?

All brothers and sisters can be embarrassing at times, whether they have autism or not!

The trouble is, most people do not know about autism and so might misunderstand what your brother or sister is trying to do or say. This is when you need to educate them! The

more people understand about autism, the more relaxed they will be.

You could explain to your friends that your brother or sister was born with autism and that it is a 'developmental disability' – he or she is not stupid, but just has problems with certain things. You could make suggestions that might help your friends and your brother or sister get along:

- 'He/she might not answer you as he/she has difficulty making sentences.'
- 'He/she does not always speak, so points to what he/she wants instead.'
- 'He/she might not always understand what you are saying, so talk clearly and in short sentences.'
- 'He/she switches off sometimes and likes to daydream.'
- 'Sometimes he/she gets upset and does not know how to tell someone.'
- 'He/she sometimes talks to him/herself because he/she forgets that we can hear.'
- 'He/she finds it hard to join in as he/she does not understand rules or about sharing or winning games.'
- 'He/she is not being naughty, it is just that he/she is not sure what to do and gets confused.'
- 'It helps if you give my brother/sister lots of time to understand and answer you.'

By explaining these points to your friends, they will immediately feel more informed. Knowledge always puts people at ease and enables them to join in with more confidence. You may think of your brother or sister as the awkward one who is unable to communicate, but, in actual fact, it could be your friends! So, guide them and help them to feel at ease – it will not be long before they are teaching other people about autism.

Always talk with respect about your brother or sister to other people – even if he or she has been really annoying you! Encourage others to do the same. Your brother or sister might not be able to stand up for him or herself.

Talk about your brother or sister as you would like other people to talk about you and you will not go far wrong.

Part 5
Special help – schools and therapies

Your brother or sister might need extra help at school or getting to school. If he or she goes to an ordinary (mainstream) school, probably some extra help will be given by an adult assistant in the classroom.

Your brother or sister might go to a special school where all the pupils have autism. Some schools have a mixture of pupils with autism and other learning difficulties.

It could be that your brother or sister is home-schooled.

As every person with autism is different, different schools will suit different pupils' needs.

The good thing about being in a general education classroom (with extra help) is that your brother or sister will learn to cope with lots of people, busy classes and lots of noise. This is a real-life situation. The extra help will probably come from one assistant who works beside your brother or sister and helps in some or all the lessons.

Your brother or sister might find that this works and is happy in this environment. For lots of people with autism, though, being at a general education classroom could be very difficult. They would find the noise overwhelming, the big classes terrifying and the whole experience very confusing.

Because of this, there are special classrooms to help people like your brother or sister learn in a way that suits him or her best. We call these resource rooms or self-contained classrooms. These classes are much smaller, with lots of staff and the ways of teaching used are ones that your brother or sister will be able to understand.

Some children with autism go to special schools. There are different types of schools that help people with autism learn as much as they can, in their own time.

Every pupil in the school has their own individual way of learning and every member of staff teaches them in this special way. This may include using words, photographs, pictures and sign language.

The teachers will organize whatever your brother or sister needs to help him or her learn. All the staff will understand about any difficulties and worries your brother or sister might have. They will work towards helping him or her overcome these fears and difficulties.

The lessons are delivered at a slower pace, so that your brother or sister does not become confused or frustrated. The classrooms and corridors might be changed to help your brother or sister learn and move around independently. Lots of things will be clearly marked with words or photographs. The classes will be kept uncluttered and as peaceful as possible. Any changes will be clearly explained to your brother or sister in advance, in a way that he or she can understand. They may make your brother or sister a set of communication cards specially. They may create an individual timetable for your brother or sister for the day, rather than make him or her follow a whole-class schedule.

All these things can make a great difference to the way your brother or sister feels at school. If he or she is feeling relaxed and safe, the classrooms are clear, he or she knows what is happening next and, when that ends, what comes after, your brother or sister is far more likely to be able to learn and enjoy time spent at school.

Therapies

What are they?

A therapy is a gentle, relaxed way of helping or healing people. Various therapies are usually used with people who have special educational needs.

In a therapy, no pressure is put on anyone – people are free to do things in their own way in their own time. Those receiving a therapy are encouraged to feel comfortable and relaxed. In time, they are able to express any fears or worries as a result of the therapy.

There are several types of therapy used with people who have autism. Here are some of the most common ones.

Speech and language therapy

Speech therapy is used to help people who have lost the ability to speak or have not learned how to use their voice or mouth to make sounds and talk.

This might include special exercises to do with the voice or learning how to make shapes with the lips and tongue. Speech therapists can work out the best ways in which your brother or sister can communicate. This might be speaking and learning new words, using pictures or sign language, whatever suits him or her best.

Speech therapists might also teach how to take turns in speaking, how to be in a group and how to listen to other people.

Art therapy

In art therapy, your brother or sister might explore the feel
and texture of materials. He or she might not actually want
to create a work of art and there is no pressure to do this.
The materials are used to help him or her relax and
experiment.

Because there are no 'rights' or 'wrongs' in art, you can
never make a mistake! Everything in art therapy is an
achievement, a success. This is encouraging for people
with autism and develops their confidence and
independence, as well as having a calming effect.

Some people with autism are able to use art as a way of
talking about their worries and concerns. They might
discuss their painting with the art therapist in private. The
pupil and art therapist look, think and talk about what is
happening in the painting, then try to work out what it
might mean.

Music therapy

Music therapy is not the same as music lessons. It is not about learning instruments or songs or reading music. It is mainly about using sound, rhythm and tempo (speed) to express feelings and encourage communication.

A music therapist will usually play the piano while your brother or sister is encouraged to play any of several musical instruments. These are usually chime bars, drums, cymbals, bells, tambourines, shakers or gongs. There is no pressure on him or her to play a particular instrument.

While playing the piano, the music therapist listens carefully to what your brother or sister is doing and follows his or her speed and style of playing. The 'tunes' are made up as they go along and the therapist and your brother or sister then have a sort of 'musical conversation'.

This can be great fun and encourages your brother or sister to listen and be aware of other people (the therapist) and him or herself.

Drama therapy

In drama therapy, your brother or sister will be able to act out how he or she feels.

He or she might use hats, masks or scarves as a disguise or pretend to be someone else. He or she may prefer to sit or lie on the floor covered in silky sheets or roll into a ball and listen to gentle music.

Sometimes, huge parachutes are used in groups to billow into the air, making tents to run about under.

Drama therapists will not put any pressure on your brother or sister – it is all about doing your own thing, in your own way, in your own time. This type of therapy aims to encourage pupils with autism to express more of themselves, which they might find easier if they are acting or in disguise.

Sensory rooms

The word 'sensory' comes from 'senses', meaning our five senses. I am sure you know that these are seeing, hearing, smelling, touching and tasting.

A sensory room is a room full of things that affect our senses. The room might be dimly lit with changing coloured fairy lights, it might have soft, colourful shapes and patterns projected on to a wall. It will probably be full of cushions, beanbags, soft mats and comfortable textures. There may be a sound board, which is a wall that, when touched, makes different sounds or plays music. The smell of perfumed oils (lavender, lemon) might be released into the air to create a calm atmosphere.

Sensory rooms are very relaxing places to be in. They are dream-like and calm. Some people with autism find them relaxing and safe and enjoy having the feeling of control they get from making lights and sounds change by touching the surfaces. Most people love to just lie on the big cushions and enjoy the magical colours, lights, sounds and sensations.

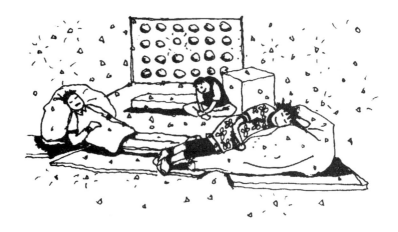

You!

So, life can be tough at times, but, just by being yourself, you are helping your brother or sister learn about the world. He or she will, in time, get used to the idea that we all need people and that other people are important.

By sharing time with you, your brother or sister will get to know you in his or her own way – the sound of your voice, the way you move, the television programs you like to watch. Although you may sometimes feel that you are unnoticed by him or her, the opposite is the case. You will always be an important part of your brother or sister's life, even if he or she is never able to say this to you.

Remember, time spent with your brother or sister is never wasted. Over the years, you will:

- develop a very patient, caring and thoughtful personality
- gain a greater understanding of people and how they think
- acquire an envious knack for solving problems
- be more able to understand your feelings and the feelings of people with and without disabilities.

Understanding your own feelings and emotions, as well as those of other people, is one of the best skills in life you can acquire. You are now halfway there.

Part 6
Glossary

Here is a list of words to do with autism and what they mean.

A

Able Having good skills/abilities
Age appropriate Something that suits the actual age of a person, not their 'mental age'
Appropriate Suitable
Art therapy A way of using art to help someone with a disability or illness
Asperger syndrome A form of autism where people generally have fewer learning difficulties than those with classic autism
Autism A developmental, social and communication disability
Autistic spectrum The full range of types of autism

B
Behaviour The way we act or behave

C

Calming behaviour Behaviour which helps someone become less tense
Challenging behaviour Behaviour that is antisocial and hurtful.

Communication Expressing ourselves with the aim that others understand us

Communication skills The ability to communicate

D

Developmental Growing and learning

Disability Lacking an ability that others usually have

Drama therapy A way of using drama and acting to help someone with a disability or illness

E

Echolalic From the word 'echo'. Used to describe the behaviour of repeating words

Empathy Understanding how someone else feels

Eye contact Looking at people during conversations

Epilepsy A condition affecting the brain that causes short losses of concentration or consciousness

F

Facial expressions Using our faces to show feelings, for example, winking, smiling, poking our tongues out

Flapping Moving hands, arms, paper and so on quickly back and forth

G

Genetic From 'genes'. Means inherited

Gestures Using our hands, arms or head to say something without using words

I

Imagination Being able to think up or make up a scene in our minds

Independence skills The ability to do this without help **Interaction** Being with other people; the way we behave with people; our approach to people

L

Learning difficulties Problems with learning

Learning disabilities Same as learning difficulties

M

Mainstream school An ordinary school that most young people go to, not one, for example, that is only for those with learning difficulties

Music therapy A way of using music to help people with a disability or illness

N

NAS The National Autistic Society of Britain

Negative attention Being noticed as a result of bad behaviour

O

Obsessive behaviour Something done over and over again which seems to have too important a place in someone's life

R

Ritualistic behaviour Always doing something in exactly the same order or in the same way

S

Sensory room A room full of coloured lights, sounds and smells used to help people with a disability or illness

Seizure A sudden blackout or faint, usually as a result of having epilepsy

Self-harm Deliberately hurting yourself

Self-injurious Self-harming

Sign language Communication by using hand signs

Signing Using hand signs instead of talking

Social To do with people and society

Socializing Making friends, being friendly, meeting people

Society All the people living in a town, city or country

Special needs Needing extra help to learn
Speech and language therapy Special classes that
help people speak or communicate
Symbols Pictures representing a thing or an idea,
sometimes used in signs

T

Targeting Choosing the same thing or person every
time
Therapy A gentle, relaxed way of helping people
feel better
Tic A movement in the face or body when the
muscles contract suddenly, and without warning
Triad of impairment The three main difficulties for
people with autism. These are in the areas of
communication, interaction and imagination

V

Visual prompts Objects, photographs, drawings –
used to help someone understand

For more information or advice about autism, you
can contact the Asperger Syndrome Coalition of
America, the Autism Society of America, Maap
Services, Inc., or the National Autistic Society of
Britain (see Useful Addresses).

Useful addresses

Asperger Syndrome
Coalition of the United
States (ASC-US)
PO Box 351268
Jacksonville, FL 32235-
1265
Tel: 864 4 ASPRGR
www.asperger.org

The National
Autistic Society (NAS)
Head Office
393 City Road
London EC1V 1NG
Tel: 020 7833 2299
www.nas org.uk

The Autism Society of
America (ASA)
7910 Woodmont Avenue
Suite 300
Bethesda, MD 20814-3067
Tel:301 657 0881
www.autism-society.org

NAS Wales
William Knox House
Suite C1
Britannic Way
Llandarcy
Neath SA10 6EL
Tel: 01792 815 915

Maap Services, Inc.
Box 524
Crown Point, IN 46308
Tel: 219 662 1311
www.maapservices.org

NAS Scotland
Central Chambers
109 Hope Street
Glasgow G2 6LL
Tel: 0141 221 8090

Index